Writing for *Challenger 3*

Skill-building writing exercises for each lesson in *Challenger 3*
of the *Challenger Adult Reading Series*

McVey & Associates, Inc.

NEW READERS PRESS

ISBN 1-56420-012-4

Copyright © 1994
New Readers Press
Publishing Division of Laubach Literacy International
Box 131, Syracuse, New York 13210-0131

Printed in the United States of America

9 8 7 6 5

 This book is printed on 100% recycled paper.

Contents

Challenger 3 ⸻

Challenger 3
Lesson 1 _____

1 **Use These Words in Sentences.** Use some of the words below to write three sentences that tell something about the story "Steven Takes Some Advice."

advice   business   driving   exercise

pact   rut   sore   temper   tense   visits

1. _____

   _____

2. _____

   _____

3. _____

   _____

2 **What Do You Think?** Complete the sentences with words that tell what you think.

1. A job that makes me feel tense is _____

   _____

2. When I feel tense and need to relax, I _____

   _____

3. Sometimes I lose my temper when _____

   _____

4. When I want to exercise, I _____

   _____

3 Combine the Sentences. Combine each pair of sentences below to make one sentence.

1. I put the dirty dishes in a dishpan. Then I washed the dishes.

   _____

2. Today's newspaper had a story. The story was about a plan that backfired.

   _____

3. The sidewalk in front of my house is broken. The city will fix the sidewalk.

   _____

4. Many workers use toolboxes. They carry in their toolboxes the tools they need to do their jobs.

   _____

   _____

4 Complete These Paragraphs. Complete the following paragraphs in your own words.

1. Steven's sister Ruth told him he should go out more, do things, and meet some new

   people. I think Ruth's advice was _____

   _____

   _____

   _____

2. People who sit a lot at their jobs can get stiff and sore. Some things they can do to feel

   better are _____

   _____

   _____

   _____

Challenger 3
Lesson 2 _____

1 **Use These Words in Sentences.** Use some of the words below to write three sentences that tell something about the story "Meet Jerome."

confused   crazy   exercise   mistake   peaceful

perched   splurge   stew   stunt   yoga

1. _____

_____

2. _____

_____

3. _____

_____

2 **What Do You Think?** Complete the sentences with words that tell what you think.

1. If I saw a friend standing on his head, I would think _____

_____

2. I think exercise is good for people because _____

_____

3. One good change I could make in my life is _____

_____

4. Classes can help people _____

_____

❸ Put These Sentences in Order. Write these sentences in the correct time order on the lines below.

Jerome was feasting on beef stew.

Steven treated Jerome to a steak dinner.

Steven was standing on his head.

Jerome said he did not think Steven was crazy.

1. _____

2. _____

3. _____

4. _____

❹ Complete These Paragraphs. Complete the following paragraphs in your own words.

1. Steven took a yoga class by mistake. He couldn't tell Jerome the difference between a

   yoga class and an exercise class because _____

   _____

   _____

   _____

2. Steven was standing on his head in the middle of his bedroom. His face had a very

   peaceful look because he _____

   _____

   _____

3. Steven cared what Jerome thought because Jerome was his best friend. Steven was glad

   Jerome did not laugh at him, so he _____

   _____

   _____

7

Challenger 3
Lesson 3 _____

1 **Use These Words in Sentences.** Use some of the words below to write three sentences that tell something about the story "Jerome Makes a Trip to the Library."

book   braced   clenching   flirt   glasses

Harvey   health   kicked   library   vowed   yogurt

1. _____

_____

2. _____

_____

3. _____

_____

2 **What Do You Think?** Complete the sentences with words that tell what you think.

1. One way to learn about something is to read a book from the library. I would read a book

from the library if I wanted to learn about _____

_____

_____

2. There are many ways to learn about things. Three other ways to learn new things are

_____

_____

_____

3 **Combine the Sentences.** Combine each pair of sentences below to make one sentence.

1. Divers use flashlights. They use flashlights to see in deep water.

   _____

2. You can use these folders. Your reports can be filed in these folders.

   _____

3. Students use notebooks. They use notebooks to write down important information.

   _____

4. Swimmers use towels. Swimmers need to dry off when they come out of the pool.

   _____

   _____

4 **Complete These Paragraphs.** Complete the following paragraphs in your own words.

1. Jerome had not been in a library since Mrs. Harvey had kicked him out of the high school

   library. Jerome thought that people who worked in libraries were _____

   _____

   _____

   _____

2. Jerome thought Steven should stop taking yoga lessons. He wanted to talk Steven out of

   going to yoga classes, but first he _____

   _____

   _____

   _____

Challenger 3
Lesson 4 _____

1 **Use These Words in Sentences.** Use some of the words below to write three sentences that tell something about the story "The Phone Call."

clowning   Ginger   hung up   improve   pigpen

relax   rude   screaming   throbbing   yoga

1. _____

_____

2. _____

_____

3. _____

_____

2 **What Do You Think?** Complete the answers to the questions with words that tell what you think.

1. How do you get along with a grouchy person? I get along with a grouchy person by

_____

_____

_____

2. What kinds of things make you feel better when you are grouchy? Things that make me

feel better are _____

_____

_____

_____

3 **Put These Sentences in Order.** Write these sentences in the correct time order on the lines below.

"I always come over to your place," complained Jerome.

Jerome let the phone ring eight times.

Ginger hung up while Jerome was still talking.

Ginger asked Jerome if he was coming over.

1. _____

2. _____

3. _____

4. _____

4 **Complete These Paragraphs.** Complete the following paragraphs in your own words.

1. Jerome started to explain yoga to Ginger, but he ended up joking about it. Ginger

   probably _____

   _____

   _____

2. Ginger hung up when Jerome didn't stop clowning around. Jerome probably _____

   _____

   _____

   _____

3. When someone clowns around on the telephone with me, I _____

   _____

   _____

   _____

Challenger 3
Lesson 5 _____

1 **Use These Words in Sentences.** Use some of the words below to write three sentences that tell something about the story "Who Is Ginger?"

    bank   hardware   homey   land   lessons   money

    owned   saved   singer   store   thrift   truthful

1. _____

   _____

2. _____

   _____

3. _____

   _____

2 **What Do You Think?** Complete the answers to the questions with words that tell what you think.

1. Why do you think Ginger doesn't spend much money on her home? I think Ginger

   doesn't spend much because _____

   _____

   _____

   _____

2. Do you think you could be as thrifty as Ginger? I think _____

   _____

   _____

   _____

3 **Combine the Sentences.** Combine each pair of sentences below to make one sentence.

1. Anne was madly in love. She was in love with Ben and wanted to marry him.

   _____

   _____

2. The boxer swung wildly. He slipped and fell against the ropes.

   _____

3. John had been away a lot lately. We hadn't seen him for a while.

   _____

4 **Complete These Paragraphs.** Complete the following paragraphs in your own words.

1. Ginger's grandmother helped her learn about thrift. I know Ginger was thrifty because

   she _____

   _____

   _____

2. I think saving money is smart. I would like to save a lot, but sometimes I _____

   _____

   _____

   _____

3. I want to save money for certain things. I'd like _____

   _____

   _____

   _____

Challenger 3
Lesson 6 _____

1 Use These Words in Sentences. Use some of the words below to write three sentences that tell something about the story "A Strange Twist of Fate."

      apartment   counter   fingers   loose   mess   oozing

      paint   paycheck   snatch   tilted   Tony   wiped

1. _____

   _____

2. _____

   _____

3. _____

   _____

2 What Do You Think? Complete the answers to the questions with words that tell what you think.

1. Why did Jerome reach for the can of blue paint? Jerome reached for the can of blue paint

   because _____

   _____

   _____

2. Why do you think it took seven hours to clean up the mess? I think it took seven hours to

   clean up the mess because _____

   _____

   _____

   _____

3 **Put These Sentences in Order.** Write these sentences in the correct time order on the lines below.

> Tony laughed so hard that he nearly slipped on the paint.
>
> Jerome reached for the can.
>
> Jerome thought about snatching a can of blue paint.
>
> Five gallons of blue paint poured over him.

1. _____

2. _____

3. _____

4. _____

4 **Complete These Paragraphs.** Complete the following paragraphs in your own words.

1. Jerome thought about snatching the paint and paying for it out of his next week's

   paycheck. If he did that, Jerome might have a problem because_____

   _____

   _____

2. Jerome thought about giving Ginger a gift of paint so that she would talk to him again.

   Giving gifts to people when they are angry is_____

   _____

   _____

3. Spilled paint makes a huge mess that is hard to clean off papers and clothes. Other things

   that make a mess are _____

   _____

   _____

15

Challenger 3
Lesson 7 _____

1 **Use These Words in Sentences.** Use some of the words below to write
three sentences that tell something about the story "At Yoga Class."

certain   chocolate   coffee   cold   exercises   involved

knack   nasty   restless   stress   sugar   unhealthy

1. _____

_____

2. _____

_____

3. _____

_____

2 **What Do You Think?** Answer these questions in complete sentences
that tell what you think.

1. Steven forgot about his cold during the yoga class. Do you feel better when you exercise?

Why or why not? _____

_____

_____

2. People eat many kinds of foods. Which foods that you eat are healthy for you? Which

are unhealthy? _____

_____

_____

_____

3 **Combine the Sentences.** Combine each set of sentences below to make one sentence.

1. Steven had a cold. He didn't feel well. Steven went to his yoga class anyway.

   _____

   _____

2. Holly told Steven he should not eat sugar. She said sugar makes people grouchy. She said it makes them restless, too.

   _____

   _____

3. Holly went to the yoga class for exercise. She also went to the class because it made her feel peaceful. Yoga made her more relaxed.

   _____

   _____

4 **Write a Paragraph.** Write a short paragraph about making your life more healthy. Use the questions below to guide you.

   Do you eat foods that are good for you?

   What foods could you eat that would be better for you?

   Do you get enough exercise?

   What new exercise could you do that would be good for you?

   How could your life be better if you ate better food and got more exercise?

   _____

   _____

   _____

   _____

   _____

   _____

Challenger 3
Lesson 8 _____

1 **Use These Words in Sentences.** Use some of the words below to write three sentences that tell something about the story "Ginger Gives Some Advice."

bragging   bruises   expect   folks   greed

mailman   proud   slouched   temper   think about

1. _____

_____

2. _____

_____

3. _____

_____

2 **What Do You Think?** Answer these questions in complete sentences that tell what you think.

1. Gail went to Ginger's apartment because she didn't want to be alone. Do you think Gail

also thought Ginger could help her? How? _____

_____

_____

2. Gail said her father gets angry when she drops by his house. How did Ginger help Gail

understand her father's anger? _____

_____

_____

3 **Put These Sentences in Order.** Write these sentences in the correct
time order on the lines below.

"You know very well your father's proud of his job," said Ginger.

Gail slouched against Ginger's doorway.

"Go wash your face, and I'll fix you some breakfast," Ginger said.

"My father lost his temper," Gail said.

"Is it okay if I stay here for a day or two?" asked Gail.

1. _____

2. _____

3. _____

4. _____

5. _____

4 **Write a Paragraph.** Write a short paragraph about giving advice to
friends. Use the questions below to guide you.

What kinds of advice do you sometimes give your friends?

When do you give advice to your friends?

Are there times when you decide not to give advice? Give an example.

Are you sometimes able to help a friend think of new ways to look at things?

How does your advice help your friends with their problems?

_____

_____

_____

_____

_____

_____

_____

Challenger 3

1 **Use These Words in Sentences.** Use some of the words below to write three sentences that tell something about the story "A Phone Call from a Friend."

bookworm   cookbook   forgive   grudge   invited   lousy

loyalty   party   sample   sandwiches   sorry   treat

1. _____

_____

2. _____

_____

3. _____

_____

2 **What Do You Think?** Answer these questions in complete sentences that tell what you think.

1. Jerome had not seen Ginger for four weeks. Do you think Jerome should have called

Ginger? Why or why not? _____

_____

_____

2. Jerome made fun of Steven's yoga class. Why do you think he did this? _____

_____

_____

_____

3 Combine the Sentences. Combine each set of sentences below to make one sentence.

1. The beef was frozen. I left it out to thaw. Then I used it to make a stew.

_____

_____

2. Bob has written a book. The book is about dogs. The book is selling well.

_____

_____

3. Joyce stopped to loosen the straps. The straps were too tight. The straps were on her backpack.

_____

_____

4 Write a Paragraph. Write a short paragraph about the way to treat friends. Use the questions below to guide you.

Would you try to help a friend who is sad? Why or why not?

What might you do to help a friend who is sad?

Would you expect your friend to do anything for you in return?

How would you expect to feel after helping a friend?

_____

_____

_____

_____

_____

_____

_____

Challenger 3
Lesson 10 _____

1 **Use These Words in Sentences.** Use some of the words below to write three sentences that tell something about the story "Jerome Goes to the Laundromat."

    clothes   fault   jerk   laundromat   losing   machines

    quarters   remember   search   slot   straightened out

1. _____

_____

2. _____

_____

3. _____

_____

2 **What Do You Think?** Answer these questions in complete sentences that tell what you think.

1. Jerome didn't like going to the laundromat. How do you feel about going to laundromats?

_____

_____

_____

2. Holly told Jerome he was a jerk. Do you agree? Why or why not? _____

_____

_____

_____

3 Put These Sentences in Order. Write these sentences in the correct time order on the lines below.

Jerome found Holly at the laundromat.

Jerome said women stick together like glue.

Holly said that Jerome is a jerk.

Jerome told Holly that Ginger should say she is sorry.

Jerome threw his laundry in the trunk of his car.

1. _____

2. _____

3. _____

4. _____

5. _____

4 Write a Paragraph. Write a short paragraph about doing laundry. Use the questions below to guide you.

Do you do your own laundry or does someone else do it for you?

Are your clothes washed in your home or at a laundromat?

Are your clothes dried in a machine or are they hung up to dry?

Who irons your clothes and puts them away?

Is this the best way to do your laundry or is there a better way?

_____

_____

_____

_____

_____

_____

_____

Challenger 3
Lesson 11 _____

1 **Use These Words in Sentences.** Use some of the words below to write three sentences that tell something about the story "The Camping Trip."

berserk   camping   daydreaming   growling   hiked   listen

nervous   newspaper   path   phone   spied   wild animal

1. _____

_____

2. _____

_____

3. _____

_____

2 **What Do You Think?** Answer these questions in complete sentences that tell what you think.

1. Do you think Ginger would be scared to camp alone again? _____

_____

2. Why do you think the fishermen might have thought Ginger was nuts? _____

_____

_____

3. Why did Ginger say she would buy a phone for every room, paint all the walls, and read

every single newspaper she could find? _____

_____

_____

3 Combine the Sentences. Combine each set of sentences below to make one sentence.

1. I don't recall my first party. I remember my first dance. I remember my first date.

   _____

   _____

2. Sam often sounds edgy. He sounds that way the first time he talks to a woman. He sounds edgy because women make him nervous.

   _____

   _____

3. Mike doesn't like to brag about things he does well. Mary wants people to know how good Mike is. She boasts for him.

   _____

   _____

4 Write a Paragraph. Write a short paragraph about camping. Use the questions below to guide you.

> If you were going camping, what food would you take?
>
> Would you take a tent and a sleeping bag?
>
> What tools would you take with you? Why would you take them?
>
> Would you want to camp alone or with a friend? Why?

_____

_____

_____

_____

_____

_____

_____

Challenger 3
Lesson 12 _____

1 **Use These Words in Sentences.** Use some of the words below to write
three sentences that tell something about the story "The Football Game."

     coach   excited   flag   football   passes   popcorn

     sulking   supposed   teams   touchdowns   ulcers   warm up

1. _____

_____

2. _____

_____

3. _____

_____

2 **What Do You Think?** Answer these questions in complete sentences
that tell what you think.

1. Holly asked if she and Steven could sit behind the batter's box. Why did Steven then say

he thought it would be a long afternoon? _____

_____

_____

2. Holly said the coach must have ulcers. What did the coach do to make her say this?

_____

_____

_____

3 Put These Sentences in Order. Write these sentences in the correct time order on the lines below.

> Buttered popcorn spilled all over Steven.
>
> Holly said, "The game is starting."
>
> Steven bought buttered popcorn.
>
> The man next to Steven bumped him.
>
> The players came onto the field.

1. _____

2. _____

3. _____

4. _____

5. _____

4 Write a Paragraph. Write a short paragraph about sports. Use the questions below to guide you.

> Which sports, if any, do you like to watch?
>
> Why do you like (or not like) to watch certain sports?
>
> Which sports, if any, do you like to play?
>
> Why do you like (or not like) to play certain sports?
>
> Which do you enjoy more, watching sports or playing them? Why?

_____

_____

_____

_____

_____

_____

_____

Challenger 3
Lesson 13 _____

1 **Use These Words in Sentences.** Use some of the words below to write
three sentences that tell something about the story "Jerome's Scheme."

     apartment   cleaned   dancing   excited   invite   party

     sadness   scheme   shopping binge   waiting   waved

1. _____

   _____

2. _____

   _____

3. _____

   _____

2 **What Do You Think?** Answer these questions in complete sentences
that tell what you think.

1. Jerome thought that getting Ginger to his party would help straighten things out. Do you

   think it was a good idea? Why or why not? _____

   _____

   _____

2. Jerome threw himself onto his bed because he was feeling sorry for himself. Do you

   think that was a grownup way to act? Why or why not? _____

   _____

   _____

   _____

3 **Combine the Sentences.** Combine each set of sentences below to make one sentence.

1. Jerome had a scheme. The scheme involved Tony. Ginger was involved in the scheme, too.

    _____

    _____

2. Jerome bought bug spray. He swept the cobwebs from the ceiling. He cleaned the carpet.

    _____

    _____

3. Anne Clark was at the party. She asked Jerome to dance. Jerome waved her away.

    _____

    _____

4 **Write a Paragraph.** Write a short paragraph about planning a party. Use the questions below to guide you.

   What kind of party do you want to plan?

   Who will you invite to the party?

   What will you have to eat and drink at the party?

   What will you do during the party?

   Will everyone have a good time?

    _____

    _____

    _____

    _____

    _____

    _____

Challenger 3
Lesson 14 _____

1 **Use These Words in Sentences.** Use some of the words below to write three sentences that tell something about the story "Whatever Happened to Tony and Ginger?"

avoided   buzz saw   charges   chestnut   complain

deed   fought   motel   neighbor   property   salesman

1. _____

_____

2. _____

_____

3. _____

_____

2 **What Do You Think?** Answer these questions in complete sentences that tell what you think.

1. Would you live the way Mr. and Mrs. Darkpill lived if you had a family problem? Why

or why not? _____

_____

_____

_____

2. How do you think Tony should treat Mrs. Darkpill? _____

_____

_____

_____

3 **Put These Sentences in Order.** Write these sentences in the correct time order on the lines below.

Tony heard the sound of a buzz saw.

Mrs. Darkpill called the police.

Mrs. Darkpill complained about the chestnut tree.

Tony yelled at Mrs. Darkpill's kids.

Tony bought a small house.

1. _____

2. _____

3. _____

4. _____

5. _____

4 **Write a Paragraph.** Write a short paragraph using the questions below to guide you.

Think of someone you know who is like Mrs. Darkpill.

What problems have you or other people had with that person?

How did you or other people handle a problem with that person?

Was that the best way to handle the problem or were there better ways to handle it?

_____

_____

_____

_____

_____

_____

_____

_____

Challenger 3
Lesson 15 _____

1 **Use These Words in Sentences.** Use some of the words below to write three sentences that tell something about the story "Mrs. Darkpill."

barged   cupboard   driveway   exciting   fight

frightened   headquarters   keyboard   neighbor   police

1. _____

    _____

2. _____

    _____

3. _____

    _____

2 **What Do You Think?** Answer these questions in complete sentences that tell what you think.

1. What do you think Mrs. Darkpill really wanted when she came to Tony's house?

    _____

    _____

2. Why do you think Tony tried to stop Ginger from talking to Mrs. Darkpill?

    _____

    _____

3. Do you think Ginger was making fun of Mrs. Darkpill? Explain your answer.

    _____

    _____

3 **Combine the Sentences.** Combine each set of sentences below to make one sentence.

1. Gail had a baby girl. The baby was born last month. The baby weighed seven pounds, eleven ounces.

_____

_____

2. I take dancing lessons. My lessons last for one hour. I go once a week.

_____

_____

3. I went to the store yesterday. I bought one quart of milk. I bought a pint of soda, too.

_____

_____

4 **Write a Paragraph.** Write a short paragraph using the questions below to guide you.

If you had been Tony, how would you have handled Mrs. Darkpill?

Would you have let her come into the house or not?

Would you have tried to talk with her?

Would you have asked Ginger to go to another room while you talked with Mrs. Darkpill?

What would you have done?

_____

_____

_____

_____

_____

_____

Challenger 3
Lesson 16 _____

1 **Use These Words in Sentences.** Use some of the words below to write three sentences that tell something about the story "Testing Recipes."

awful   behave   commit   complex   judge

oven   prunes   recipe   rules   taste   wisecracks

1. _____

_____

2. _____

_____

3. _____

_____

2 **What Do You Think?** Answer these questions in complete sentences that tell what you think.

1. Holly tore up her recipe card for prune whip. Why do you think she did this?

_____

_____

_____

2. Holly says that Jerome won't do what he should to get what he wants in life. What do you think she means by that? Explain your answer. _____

_____

_____

_____

3 Combine the Sentences. Combine each set of sentences below to make one sentence.

1. The elbow is a joint in the body. Another is the knee. The wrist is a joint, too.

   _____

   _____

2. We have a new bathroom. The bathroom has a towel rack. It also has a shower.

   _____

   _____

3. Martin is a good bowler. He is on a bowling team. The team bowls every Thursday.

   _____

   _____

4 Write a Paragraph. Write a short paragraph using the questions below to guide you.

   Do you think Jerome is right or wrong?

   Do you think he should call Ginger now that he knows what really happened?

   Why or why not?

   _____

   _____

   _____

   _____

   _____

   _____

   _____

   _____

Challenger 3
Lesson 17 _____

1 **Use These Words in Sentences.** Use some of the words below to write three sentences that tell something about the story "Tony's Day Off."

booth   breakfast   clothing   comply   curtain   desire

dock   Mr. Dennis   pay   quiet   sick   unfriendly

1. _____

_____

2. _____

_____

3. _____

_____

2 **What Do You Think?** Answer these questions in complete sentences that tell what you think.

1. Why do you think Tony wanted to call in sick? _____

_____

_____

2. Why did Tony want to tell his boss off? _____

_____

_____

3. What should Tony have done that day? Explain your answer. _____

_____

_____

3 **Put These Sentences in Order.** Write these sentences in the correct time order on the lines below.

Tony chose two pairs of slacks to try on.

Mr. Dennis fired Tony.

Tony went to the clothing sale at the men's store.

Tony shut off the alarm.

Tony told the person in the fitting booth to hurry up.

Tony told Mr. Dennis he was sick.

1. _____

2. _____

3. _____

4. _____

5. _____

6. _____

4 **Write a Paragraph.** Write a short paragraph using the questions below to guide you.

Do you think it is right or wrong to call in sick when you are not really sick?

Are there times when you think it is all right and other times when it is wrong?

Do you think it hurts anybody else when you are not there?

Give reasons for your answers.

_____

_____

_____

_____

_____

_____

_____

Challenger 3
Lesson 18 _____

1 **Use These Words in Sentences.** Use some of the words below to write three sentences that tell something about the story "A Talk with Jerome."

complaining   disagree   disgusted   exhausted   garbage

important   limit   mistake   preach   straightened out   upset

1. _____

_____

2. _____

_____

3. _____

_____

2 **What Do You Think?** Answer these questions in complete sentences that tell what you think.

1. Jerome felt Steven was being too harsh with him. Why do you think Jerome felt

   this way? _____

_____

_____

2. Steven said Jerome should take a chance and call Ginger. Do you agree? Why or

   why not? _____

_____

_____

_____

3 **Combine the Sentences.** Combine each set of sentences below to make one sentence.

1. The carpenter needed some nails. She needed a saw. She had a drill.

   _____

   _____

2. A fisherman uses a rod for fishing. He uses hooks with the rod. He uses bait, also.

   _____

   _____

3. A baker uses a rolling pin. The rolling pin is used to roll out dough. The dough is put in pie plates.

   _____

   _____

4 **Write a Paragraph.** Write a short paragraph using the questions below to guide you.

       Do you think Steven's advice to Jerome was good or bad? Why?

       What might Steven have done differently?

       What would you have said to Jerome?

_____

_____

_____

_____

_____

_____

_____

Challenger 3
Lesson 19 _____

1 **Use These Words in Sentences.** Use some of the words below to write three sentences that tell something about the story "Jerome and Ginger."

bouncer   downhearted   explain   intense   lovely   murmured

nightclub   overcome   sing   underneath   uptown

1. _____

_____

2. _____

_____

3. _____

_____

2 **What Do You Think?** Answer these questions in complete sentences that tell what you think.

1. Jerome didn't feel downhearted after he decided to act. Why do you think deciding to

act helps people feel better?_____

_____

_____

_____

2. How have you confronted a problem with another person in your life? _____

_____

_____

_____

3 **Put These Sentences in Order.** Write these sentences in the correct
time order on the lines below.

Jerome sat at a table near the band.

Jerome decided to see Ginger in person.

Ginger felt Jerome's stare and looked up.

Ginger sang "September Song."

Jerome said he missed Ginger very much.

Jerome went to the club where Ginger was singing.

1. _____

2. _____

3. _____

4. _____

5. _____

6. _____

4 **Write a Paragraph.** Write a short paragraph using the questions below
to guide you.

At first Jerome lied to Ginger about why he went to her club.

Can you think of a better way for Jerome to handle his problem?

Do you think most people would do what Jerome did? Why or why not?

_____

_____

_____

_____

_____

_____

_____

Challenger 3
Lesson 20 _____

1 **Use These Words in Sentences.** Use some of the words below to write three sentences that tell something about the story "Holly Gives a Party."

bookstores   cheesecake   cookbook   contract   enjoyed
happen   Holly   pale   spaghetti   success   yoga

1. _____

_____

2. _____

_____

3. _____

_____

2 **What Do You Think?** Answer these questions in complete sentences that tell what you think.

1. Why do you think Jerome calls things like spaghetti "real food"? _____

_____

_____

_____

2. Why do you think Holly's party was a great success? _____

_____

_____

_____

3 Combine the Sentences. Combine each set of sentences below to
make one sentence.

1. Bob has a passport. The passport is from England. Bob's picture is in the passport.

   _____

   _____

2. The story of the flight of the Jews from Egypt has been told. This story is told in the Bible. It is remembered each year during Passover.

   _____

   _____

3. I carry heavy gear for camping. I use a knapsack for my gear. I carry the knapsack on my back.

   _____

   _____

4 Write a Paragraph. Write a short paragraph using the questions below
to guide you. Explain your answers.

   How do you think Jerome's and Ginger's lives will turn out?

   Do you think they will stay together for a long time?

   Do you think they will be happy together?

   Do you think they will talk with each other when they have problems instead of not speaking?

   _____

   _____

   _____

   _____

   _____

   _____

   _____

Challenger 3
Review _____

1 **Combine the Sentences.** Combine each pair of sentences below to make one sentence.

1. Ginger finally painted her apartment. She painted it blue. She hung new curtains, too.

   _____

   _____

2. Steven practiced yoga every day. He got very good at yoga. He became a yoga instructor.

   _____

   _____

3. Holly got food from the refrigerator. She cooked the food and ate her dinner. She did all of this in thirty minutes.

   _____

   _____

2 **What Do You Think?** Answer these questions in complete sentences that tell what you think.

1. Many people like to play or watch basketball. Others don't like it. Do you like the sport of basketball? Why or why not? _____

   _____

   _____

2. We are told that smoking cigarettes is unhealthy. Do you agree or disagree? Why?

   _____

   _____

3. Having a car can be a problem. A car costs a lot to buy. There are many other expenses such as gas and repairs. Yet many people have cars. Do you think it is worth having the problems to own a car? Why or why not? _____

_____

_____

_____

3 **Put These Sentences in Order.** Write these sentences in the correct time order on the lines below.

The policeman waited while Tony changed the tire.

Tony had a blowout as he drove.

Tony was only ten minutes late for his new job.

Tony thanked the policeman for keeping other cars from hitting him.

Tony drove his car to work.

Tony was fixing his flat tire when a police car stopped.

1. _____

_____

2. _____

_____

3. _____

_____

4. _____

_____

5. _____

_____

6. _____

_____

4 Write Paragraphs. Write short paragraphs using the questions below to guide you. Explain your answers.

1.   What do you like to do for amusement?

    Do you like to go to the park, to the movies, to a ball game?

    Do you like to do things alone or with other people?

    Do you like to go places with friends or with family?

_____

_____

_____

_____

_____

_____

_____

_____

_____

_____

_____

_____

_____

_____

_____

_____

_____

2.   What kind of work do you like most?

     Do you do that kind of work now?

     Are you able to do that work?

     What kind of training is needed for the work you like?

     Where did you get training for this job or where could you get the training?

     If you don't do this work now, what must you do to get the job?

     _____

     _____

     _____

     _____

     _____

     _____

     _____

     _____

     _____

     _____

     _____

     _____

     _____

     _____

     _____